ACROSS
THE
GENERATIONS

ACROSS THE GENERATIONS

THE COLLECTED WRITINGS OF RUTH LOUISE HAYES WILLIAMS

ADDITIONAL POETRY BY OSGOOD GASTON HAYES

COMPILED
by
Carol Chandler Russ
and
Betty Williams Chandler

Home Crafted Artistry & Printing
New Albany, Indiana

This publication is intended to provide poetic inspiration and consolation to the reader. The statements and opinions expressed in this book are those of the authors.

Across the Generations © 2016 by Carol Chandler Russ. The book's author retains sole copyright to this book. All rights reserved. Printed 2016 by Home Crafted Artistry & Printing with permission.

Except for brief quotations and except as permitted under the United States Copyright Act of 1976, no part of this publication may be reproduced or distributed in any form or means, printed or electronic, without written permission of the publisher or author.

Unless otherwise noted, photos are property of Carol Chandler Russ.
Cover photos: Ruth Louise Hayes Williams;
insets: Osgood Gaston Hayes; Carol Chandler Russ; Betty Williams Chandler

Proudly printed and bound in the United States of America.

ISBN-13: 978-0-9964089-8-1
ISBN-10: 0-9964089-8-3

Additional copies of this book may be purchased by visiting the E-Store for this title at:
createspace.com/6047152

Home Crafted Artistry and Printing
1252 Beechwood Avenue
New Albany, IN 47150
HomeCraftedArtistry.com

To my granddaughters,

Abigail, Rebekah, and Eliora.

May you grow in wisdom, grace, and love

and become like my grandmother,

your great-great grandmother

Louise Hayes Williams.

Carol Chandler Russ, "Nana"

CONTENTS

Introduction xi

Part One: The Collected Writings of Ruth Louise Hayes Williams

WHO WAS LOUISE HAYES WILLIAMS? 1

If Things Go Wrong 12

For the Good Cheer Class 14

Thinking of You 16

Our Betty, Four Years Old 18

I Must Learn to Give 22

On Memie's 53rd Birthday 24

The Breeze 25

Summertime   26

Autumn   28

Sunset   30

A Rainy Night   32

A Rainy Night: Ernest's Response   34

To Mama from LHW   35

Life's Like That   36

The Small Voice   38

The Williams Family Reunion   40

All is Well   43

My Prayer   44

Thanksgiving   46

Our Little Jim   48

Advice to a Young Girl   49

Emotion   50

Boy Dreams   69

A Trip to See Santa Claus   70

My Gifts to Christ at Christmas   72

To Have a Friend   73

My Morning Prayer   74

My Garden Paths   75

My Loves   76

I Wish for You   78

The Rose of Friendship   80

Content   81

Release   82

Life's Sea   83

Blessed Are God's Own   84

Thank You, God, for Life   86

Solving Problems   88

To Betty on Mother's Day 1953 From Mother   90

To Rise Again   91

Growth   92

Leave It with Him   93

I Am Glad to Live in America   95

Toward a Successful Life   103

A Prayer from the Heart of a Mother   107

Part Two: The Poetry of Osgood Gaston Hayes

WHO WAS OSGOOD HAYES?   113

Merely a Dream   116

The Day's Investments   118

The New Day   119

The Significant Hand   120

Things That Abide   122

ABOUT THE AUTHORS   123

INTRODUCTION

FROM MY EARLIEST DAYS growing up in Atlanta, Georgia, my four loving, Christian grandparents were very closely involved in my life. Mother's parents were Ernest and Louise Hayes Williams. Dad's parents were Eddie and Ezzie Webb Chandler. We sewed, cooked, went to church and school, and enjoyed family events together. We worked in the garden, visited family and friends, took trips, and had picnics. My grandparents were such a tremendous blessing from God to my two brothers, Jim and John, and me. How thankful we are to have had them! How many things our grandparents taught us! The most valuable gifts they shared were their love of family (past, present, and future) and their faith in God, which was reflected in every aspect of their lives: how they prayed about everything, how they were thankful for the most ordinary things, and how they loved people – at church; in their neighborhoods, schools, and work; and in our extended family.

It was not until 2012 that I discovered that in addition to wonderful memories, I also am blessed to have my Grandmother Louise's poems and two pieces of her prose – many in her own handwriting. In addition, I have several poems written by her father, Osgood Gaston Hayes. After my mother's death in 2010, I found notebooks of her mother's poems and prose which Mother had collected and given to family members as Christmas gifts in 1993. At the time, the thought occurred to me that someday I might want to publish them.

Then in 2014, I travelled to Basking Ridge, New Jersey, to attend the 50th anniversary celebration of the founding of Somerset Hills Baptist Church, which had been my biological family's church during the early 1970s. While there, I met David and Carolyn Dean, who had been members of the church in the 1990s. When they learned about my interest in publishing the poetry, they gave me the name of their dear editor friend Joyce Sweeney Martin, who lives less than ten miles from my home in Louisville, Kentucky. How amazing to travel 800 miles and be connected with an editor in my own backyard!

This connection to Joyce and her expertise proved to be just what I needed! With her help, I have been able to preserve for future generations the words of my grandmother and great-grandfather – words I consider to be treasures too precious to lose. I wanted to preserve and share their faith, their thoughts, and the beauty they saw in our world. *Across the Generations* has made that dream a reality.

As I reflected on my grandmother's life, I also realized that she became a grandmother at age fifty-two, which was the age at which I, too, became a grandmother. Abigail Catherine Russ, daughter of son Mark William Russ and Lauren Adcock Russ, was born in 2007. In 2011 and 2014, my husband, William, and I were blessed with two more granddaughters, Rebekah Lynn Russ, second daughter of Mark and Lauren, and Eliora Kathryn Russ, daughter of son David Chandler Russ and Deandra Hoppe Russ.

This volume helps fulfill my desire to prepare something for my children and my grandchildren that came from my own parents and grandparents ... a volume about faith, the beauty of our world, family, friendships, church, and insights on wise living. May the rich heritage of love and faith that I was given continue ACROSS THE GENERATIONS ... FROM those I loved TO those I love!

Blessings to all of you!

Carol Jane Chandler Russ
Nana / Mom / Mother / Carol
March 2016
Louisville, Kentucky

PART ONE

THE COLLECTED WRITINGS

OF

RUTH LOUISE HAYES WILLIAMS

(Born Aug. 01, 1902, Greene County, Georgia;
Died Aug. 31, 1992, Atlanta, Georgia)

WHO WAS LOUISE HAYES WILLIAMS?

By Carol Chandler Russ

BLESSED WITH COURAGE and determination arising from her deep Christian faith, my maternal grandmother Ruth Louise "Louise" Hayes Williams faced every trial that came her way with great grace and peace. As I read her poetry, I see that resilience and faith. And as I reflect on the grandmother with whom I spent many hours, I also am struck by her great sense of FUN.

I remember one occasion when "Gaga" (her 'grandmother' name), Granddad "Gops"

James Ernest Williams, and I were enroute from our home in Atlanta to a family reunion in Paris, Tennessee, to visit my grandfather's beloved brother Percy, his wife Lutie Cowan, and their family when we stopped to spend the night in a hotel. In the 1960s before America's interstate highway system was completed, a 400-mile trip often required more than one day. Even though it has been more than forty years, I can still picture the scene: After we had settled in, Gaga and I sat on the bed listening to my grandfather read from the Bible ... passionately, loudly, and late into the night. Suddenly, Gaga burst into laughter. Needless to say, my grandfather grew quite perturbed and demanded to know the reason for such unseemly behavior. Between laughs, with her eyes twinkling, Gaga assured him that she wasn't laughing at his reading the Bible; she was merely thinking of the other hotel guests. Might his loud, passionate reading not awaken them? She ventured the thought that those who heard him reading Scripture so late that night in his booming voice must have thought the Lord was returning ... RIGHT THEN!

On another occasion, when I was in college, Gaga took my mother and me on an ancestor-hunting adventure to south Alabama. An avid genealogist, Gaga left no stone unturned when searching for family roots. That time, after arriving in the small town where some of our ancestors were buried in a small family cemetery, she went to the home of distant cousins whom she had visited ten years earlier. She knew they could tell us the location of the gravel road off the two-lane blacktop where an early 1800s family cemetery lay obscured deep in a cornfield.

Instead of trying to describe the twists and turns off country roads where there were few, if any, road signs, the cousins decided it would be easier to show us. But first, they provided us with a proper country breakfast. What a feast: bacon, eggs, grits, milk gravy, biscuits! Meanwhile, they called several other people in the community who were familiar with the area. Two hours later, I found myself helping a little ninety-year-old lady over a rail fence in the middle of someone's cornfield. Believe me, that little old lady was not as frail as she looked. Nevertheless, as I pushed her up over the rail fence, I found myself praying that the Lord wouldn't choose that moment to call her home to heaven. Sure enough, we found that ancient family cemetery just where it was supposed to be. As we left the cemetery, Gaga was very happy.

But that isn't the end of that adventure. Before we had left Atlanta, at the last minute, my grandmother had traded cars with my Uncle Jim. I guess she thought his car was more suited or in better shape for the journey. What she didn't know was that the transmission had been slipping. As we set out to return to Atlanta, we soon found out. There we were, three women in rural Alabama, miles from any city, with a totally failed transmission. What to do? Gaga did what she always did in unexpected situations: She prayed hard and then took action. She called AAA.

Thankfully, the auto association found a mechanic who was willing to work all Saturday night rebuilding that transmission so we could drive home to Atlanta on Sunday afternoon and be back at work on Monday morning. AMAZING! Gaga exuded her thanks to Jesus, to AAA, and to that mechanic. She also gave him a small gift.

Looking back, I realize that people were Gaga's passion and leadership was her gift. Granted, her family – past, present, and future – were at the top of her list, but it didn't stop there. Whether with her family, at church, or in her community, throughout her life, she exercised her leadership gifts serving others. For example, my mother loved to tell the story about how Gaga – as a young mother – organized a neighborhood skating club for her and her girlfriends. Mother proudly told me about how Gaga served as PTA (Parent-Teacher Association) president at my mother's elementary school. At Second Ponce de Leon Baptist Church, Gaga was the first president of the Aliae Sunday School class in which she was a member for more than fifty years. One of her poems in this volume, "For the Good Cheer Class, In Honor of Our Mothers," was written for that class.

Gaga valued friends. In one poem in this volume, "To Have a Friend," she reflects on the importance of having friends. In another, "The Rose of Friendship," she compares the heart of a friend to the sweet fragrance of a rose. Both poems were written when Gaga was in her early forties, during the time when her beloved husband suffered two disabling heart attacks, her mother died, and other family members faced severe medical crises. In those years, she learned just how important her friends were.

Typical of the value Gaga placed on friendship was the close bond she shared with my father's mother, Ezzie Chandler, who was also a life-long member of the Aliae Sunday School class.

For Gaga, indeed life wasn't without its difficulties. Yet no matter what she faced, she was always pro-active and courageous. At age forty, when confronted with her two-year-old son's severe juvenile diabetes, her response was to organize a lay society for Atlanta-area families of diabetic children.

At age fifty, when facing my grandfather's second heart attack, she went to work to support the family. Until that time in the twenty-five-years of their marriage, Gaga had been a stay-at-home wife and mother caring for her husband, daughter Betty, and son Jim. She had also been actively involved in her church, her children's schools, and her community. And she wrote poetry. Faced with her husband's disability, for the first time in her life she entered the workforce to support her family.

For the next twenty-five years, Gaga pursued a career. Although she did not have a college degree, she assisted many years in the library of Sylvan Hills High School. She loved her work as she counseled and encouraged students.

After she retired from the school system, Gaga became director of the Diabetes Association of Atlanta. In that position, she helped countless people manage health issues. For her work, she was nominated for various awards in Atlanta and in Georgia. As a teenager and young adult, I was often amazed to see articles about my grandmother in the big-city *Atlanta Journal – Constitution* newspaper. As Gaga plunged her time and energies into these works, her poetry writing and community activities declined. Her only extant writing from her later years was written when she was eighty-two-years old. That piece, "A Prayer from the Heart of a Mother," is included in this volume. Three years after writing that, Gaga suffered a massive stroke which impaired her ability to communicate. Five years later, she died in Atlanta. (Her beloved husband had died sixteen years earlier.)

My Gaga's life enriched the lives of so many people in so many ways. I believe that when we share a person's thoughts and ideas, that person lives on. May you enjoy my Gaga's thoughts and dreams as you read her words. May she live on.

IF THINGS GO WRONG

If things go wrong as day
   is beginning
Sing your cheeriest song and keep
   on grinning.

If you are ever so blue, unhappy,
   and pining,
Clouds of dull hue will turn
   to shining.

If you manage to smile tho' your
   heart is aching
You'll set a good style
   of gloom forsaking.

If your excellent trait
   is ever showing
And on the suffering you wait,
   then character's growing.

If you kindle the glow of cheerful feeling
Then you'll banish woe as it comes stealing.

Let's guard every deed with all our being.
   And Right Living heed –
For God is All Seeing.

March 1932
Age 29

FOR THE GOOD CHEER CLASS

*To the mothers of the women
in my Sunday School class,
Second Ponce de Leon Baptist Church,
Atlanta, Georgia*

Our mothers dear
   We're glad you're here!
      Our class is yours today!

Make yourselves at ease
   Your daughters you'll please
      As we celebrate Mother's Day.

As you're here, Mrs. Knight,
   You'll rise to new heights,
      For you make us feel that way.

We're glad you came
   To our class of fame
      To be honored by us today.

You're Good Cheer Mothers
   And there are many others
      Who couldn't be here today.

As the years come and go,
   We'll ever love you so,
      The same as we do today.

May 1932
Age 29

THINKING OF YOU

Night is drawing near
    And your spirit so dear
        Catches hold of my heart.

You are close in my thoughts
    For long I have sought
        Someone like you to adore.

As twilight comes on
    New dreams are born
        Of my making for you.

I wonder what you're thinking
    As day is fast sinking
        Could you be dreaming of me?

You may not care
    That in my heart I share
        Your sweetest thoughts with you.

Yet I feel that you do
    That's why I'm not blue
        Thinking my thoughts of you.

June 1932
Age 29

OUR BETTY, FOUR YEARS OLD

Hopefully, she'll be wholesome,
    And loving and true;
To all, to honor and giving
    Of herself all that is due.

If she'll always be truthful
    Faithful to every trust
Ever thoughtful of others –
    She'll be a pleasure to us.

Let her know how to combat
    The adversities she will meet,
And keep a profound faith
    As she sits at Jesus' feet.

I'd have her be polite,
    Possessing a gracious way
A person of lovely manner
    Forgetting herself always.

I hope she'll love God's work
    Giving to it from her soul.
She'll catch the broader gleam
    Once His story she's told.

I want her to be healthy
    And as happy as can be
With a character so clean
    And open so all may see.

She'll need to develop patience
    And learn her turn to wait,
The good things from the bad
    She must learn to separate.

She must have a sense of humor
    If she's to get along,
For life at its very best
    Is not always a song.

I pray she'll love her friends
    And they'll be true to her.
For, with them living's easier
    Though hardships do occur.

My ambition may seem high
    But why not, I ask of you –
She's our only girl –
    And God is with us, too.

July 25, 1932
Age 20

I MUST LEARN TO GIVE

Oft time I long to be a bird,
    Able to conquer the clouds
And lose disturbing emotions –
    While happiness my soul enshrouds.

If I were a bird on wing,
    What would it matter to me
If little things went wrong –
    Away from the scene I'd be.

I wouldn't have to worry
    Though things did go wrong.
All my thoughts would be of flying
    And composing some sweet song.

I'm afraid I wouldn't be happy
    Such a narrow life to live.
It takes the sadness and pain
    To show us how to give.

Thru giving we're truly living
   For to give is to receive.
I pray that I may master this art
   Before this world I leave.

Sept. 22, 1932
Age 30

ON MEMIE'S 53rd BIRTHDAY
To my mother,
Ruth Elizabeth Williams Hayes

We intended for you to rest
So this gift will be the test,
If you have a lazy bone
We'd be so shocked we'd moan.
But how happy we would be
If right often we could see
You lounging in this gift.

It would give our hearts a lift.
Quit your work awhile and see
How comfortable you can be.
Tho' this chair is for the beach
In our yard it'll be a peach!
And if you occupy it, Memie,
You'll see our eyes grow beamy.

1932
Age 30

THE BREEZE

The billow – y, willow – y breeze,
Sings melodies through the trees,
It brushes gently past me.
As it rushes, it seems to ask me
    To come along its way.

It's pleased to tease, as it blows.
It presses and caresses as it goes.
On second thought, it returns
To soothe the sunmade burns
    But it never seems to stay.

As we treasure, find pleasure, in flowers,
Are refreshed by the freshet of showers.
The softness of the breeze in the trees,
Is retreat from the winter's freeze,
    As the night is, from the day.

We'll remember in December the glow
That wrapped us in rapture, to know
The feel, just to steal, enchanted,
To the good, cool wood God planted
    Though the breeze has gone its way.

Undated

SUMMERTIME

God's great terrain
Fresh washed by rain
And dried in the morning sun;
His flowers aglow
In glamorous show
And I know that summer's begun.

Since summer is here
I'm sure I hear
A call to bathe in the sun,
To walk in the rain,
A ramble again,
Through the woods, for summer's begun.

Undated

AUTUMN

*Read by Rev. Roy Hurst, brother
of my friend Margaret Wallace,
on his "Inspirational Corner"
radio program,
Station KTHS, Hot Springs, Arkansas
Nov. 07, 1932*

I love to stroll in the wildwood
    In the autumn of the year.
All nature seems to be resting,
    Preparing for winter so near.

There is a quiet and a stillness
    Except for the falling leaves.
The sky is as clear as crystal.
    A spell of magic the scenery weaves.

It is so nice to follow the trail
    Up and over the hill.
And before we hardly realize,
    We come to a stream so still.

A stroll in the woods is satisfying
   In the autumn days so fine.
If I had a choice of the seasons,
   I'd take these perfect days for mine.

Autumn 1932
Age 30

SUNSET

As the sun sank low in the western sky
It infused its glow in all I passed by.
It enveloped my heart with a silent awe.
It developed a beauty in all I saw.
And I see beauty when I can.

The colors of autumn ran riot in the light.
I watched them retire with the coming night.
As the sun was gone for another day,
And God in His Heaven seemed to say,
"And all is right with man."

Some golden minutes are ours each day.
They can neither be given nor taken away
But only be shared by those who can feel
The depth of nature and the things
     that are real,
God's message since the world began.

Undated

A RAINY NIGHT

*After I wrote this Christmas-season poem,
my husband, Ernest,
responded with a poem of his own.*

As the rain comes pattering on my roof,
   I'm thankful that I'm at home.
Let it pour, let it storm and thunder.
   I have no desire to roam.

There's lots of things I can do tonight.
   I can sew, I can muse as I read.
I can rummage in old papers and pictures.
   Not a call outside will I need.

There are many things I ought to do,
   Like letters I must write.
Buttons need sewing and socks
      need darning.
My work basket's really a sight!

But I settle down with a book to read
   Beneath a bright bridge lamp.
Then I remember the letter I mailed today,
   I forgot to put on a stamp.

With that out of mind, I continue to read.
    And then I suddenly remember
For Christmas, I am so unprepared,
    And it's the middle of December!

So laying aside my book with regret
    I begin to make out a list
As to what to give and why and to whom,
    And my mind is quickly all a mist.

So the rain patters down on my roof
    While these simple tasks I perform.
Someday I'll read and do as I please
    While there's rain and wind and storm.

I'm glad there's always something to do
    To engage my hand and mind
For it must be terrible for time to lag.
    As down thru life we wind.

Undated

A RAINY NIGHT: ERNEST'S RESPONSE

I think your poem is good,
    You wrote it on a rainy night.
I, too, would write if I could
    And put my thoughts in the light.

Your poem has a certain air
    I cannot soon forget.
I read it over with care
    And remember the day we met.

You seem to love your home ...
    Let's fill it with joy and glee!
You have no need to roam.
    Just stay with Betty and me.

Undated

TO MAMA FROM LHW
To my fifty-eight-year-old mother

There's nobody else on the face of the earth
    Can take the place of my mother,
She lovingly does the million things
    That I can expect from no other.

I'm first in her thought from morn til night
    And my welfare is ever on her mind,
Deep in my heart there's a constant prayer
    For my life to be as she designed.

She's endured the heartaches a mother
        goes thru;
She's thrilled over all my good luck;
She's inspired in me a determining will
    To face adversity with pluck.

Here's my prayer to my Father in Heaven –
    "In her soul let there be a peace
With ever a consciousness of my love
    A love that shall never cease."

Jan. 19, 1933
Age 30

LIFE'S LIKE THAT

Things can't always go 'long smooth
With never a ruffled feelin' to soothe.
Jus' at the time when we're so content
In our sail o' happiness, comes a rent –
That's got to have a mendin'.

Why should we expect to find only joy?
Why should we let such trifles annoy?
We human beins' can act so small
Keeping our faces turned to the wall
In our misery unbendin'.

It's jus' that way with this life we live.
For all we receive, there's a lot to give.
Jus' when we're sittin' on top o' the world
From our perch on high,
We're suddenly hurled to the earth below.

Give life a laugh an' a ready smile.
It makes the livin' more worth the while.
Remember, the folks who count stay by.
And the ones who don't – why even sigh?
Jus' let 'em go.

There have to be heartaches and sorrow
If we've anything to begin on tomorrow.
So turn your back on your mood
    and forget it
When tomorrow comes – you won't regret it
In your heart you'll grow.

April 06, 1933
Age 30

THE SMALL VOICE

Something speaks as from afar,
"You're seeing people as they are –
Not what they'd really like to be –
So, open your heart and try to see."

When someone seems so awfully rude,
Maybe his early advantages were crude,
And his chances of being somebody, few
And the finer life to him is new.

So many things could hinder him
The world is so willing to condemn.
Then all he knows to do is sigh
And think – "Why should I try?"

Let's listen to the voice and hear
And to the hearts of folks draw near
'Cause if we do, we're bound to see
These self-same folks as they'd like to be.

May 1933
Age 30

THE WILLIAMS FAMILY REUNION

The day dawned on a happy scene
Of a family united again;
The devotion of each to the other
Will forever and ever remain.

We met at sister's and brother's
And most everybody was there.
The barbecued pig was delicious.
For this day we banished care.

There was the natural fellowship,
And loads and loads of food.
Everyone did what he wanted to
And entered in as he should.

There were Percy and Lutie
    and Percy Mac
Ernest and Eunice and Jeanne.
That baby's curly hair
Is the cutest you've ever seen.

Charlie and Alma and Eloise,
    Percy, Tab, and Pauline
It's hard for one to realize
That girl is nearly sixteen.

Alberta ate so much ice cream
    We really were alarmed.
Curtis, Cecelia, and little Alberta
    Saw she was unharmed.

Albert and Salla Mae were there,
    And Claude and Jeptha, too.
They're darling little fellows
    And act so sweet, they do.

Ernest, Louise, and Betty
    Certainly enjoyed the day.
If you asked them about reunions,
    You know what they would say.

Mr. and Mrs. Sil Thompson
    And Billy and Joseph and Jim
So big and brown and healthy
    And full of vigor and vim.

There were the Ernest Vaughns
    Mr. Hayes and Mr. Seay
And when the dinner was over,
    They were as full as they could be.

The three Burns sisters came
    In fact, we had a crowd
And at this family reunion
    Only pleasure was allowed.

Two family servants stayed on the job;
    They helped wherever needed.
Aunt Francis and Gains Hollis
    Every call they heeded.

We had a gorgeous time
    And hope again to meet.
We love each other so very much,
    This reunion we must repeat.

July 04, 1933
Age 30

ALL IS WELL

So much of nature is wonderful,
   So many friends are true.
So many flowers are blooming,
   How can a fellow be blue?

So many children are laughing
   So many birds pass singing.
How can a fellow be blue,
   With so much happiness ringing?

Of course, there's sickness about
   And lots of folks are sad.
There are days of utter blackness
   And even the best looks bad.

They'll always be lots of trouble
   For those who see that side.
But there'll also be the cheerful
   Who manage to turn the tide.

Since life itself is so grand
   And it's God's first gift to me.
"Give me the character to live it
   And its better side to see."

August 1933
Age 31

MY PRAYER

Lord, give me a sense of quiet and peace
Let the noise and deadly confusion cease
And o'er my soul let a stillness be
Then keep me, Lord, so close to Thee.

Oh! Give me the poise required to meet
The clamor of life that I must defeat;
These things I crave from the depth of my soul
For a life that's serene I want to mold.

My prayer, dear Lord, at the close of this day
Is that Thou shalt show me Thine own way;
Give me the strength to face ugly things
And give me the peace Thy love alone brings.

Aug. 20, 1933
Age 31

THANKSGIVING

From deep in my heart
I give thanks this day
For the thoughts of beauty I possess,
For the air that is pure,
And the song of a bird and
    The adoration of a child's caress.

For the confidence that comes
In a stranger's glance
As he casually passes me by,
For the sermons on life
That lift me up
    And stir my soul to aspire!

I am thankful today
For the respect of man
Tho' he be but a tiny lad,
For the sympathizing tears
That I can shed
    With a friend in his hour that's sad.

Today I give thanks
For the chance to grow
In a field that is yet unsown.
The life I desire
To fashion with God
    To me heretofore unknown.

1935
Age 33

OUR LITTLE JIM
*To my four-week-old son Jim,
who still weighs less than five pounds*

Two little eyes that "ought to be" blue
And a cute little turned up nose.
Two little ears that seem so new
And the mouth like the bud of a rose.

Two little hands that he waves about
Or folds up under his chin.
It's hard to think his legs'll be stout
And walking someday among men.

He'll soon rub the hair off his head
But what does it matter to him?
He lies and sleeps in his little bed
As he grows – our little Jim.

Aug. 20, 1940
Age 38

ADVICE TO A YOUNG GIRL
To my sixteen-year-old daughter, Betty

Seek out the lovely,
The fine and the true.
Hold to the natural
And just be you.

Touch gently with deep
And understanding heart;
Then, my dear,
You'll have a good start.

It takes some sorrow,
Some suffering, to grow.
Disillusions sting,
Often we know.

There's so much fun
And happiness, too.
Always hold fast
To that which is true.

1944
Age 42

EMOTION

Have you ever stood speechless
   at the beauty of a thing?
When words seemed futile and you felt
   you must cling?
To security that keeps your feet
   on the earth
By doing or saying the thing
   of no worth –
Holding to your star awhile.

The sunset casts its radiant glow
So deep in my soul that nobody'd know,
But should I suddenly be placed
   in a crowd,
Of the beautiful sunset
   I couldn't speak aloud –
Perhaps I'd casually smile.

Have you ever had expression
    of friendship so rare
So precious to hold that you
    couldn't share,
Not even in your manner
    with the folk about,
So you pressed it down so it
    couldn't peep out –
Holding to your star awhile.

Dec. 03, 1944
Age 42

YOUNG POET, CIRCA 1930
Ruth Louise "Louise" Hayes Williams began writing poetry as a young woman.

PROUD PARENTS, CIRCA 1931
James Ernest Williams and Louise Hayes
Williams lovingly admire their daughter,
Betty Louise Williams.

HAYES FAMILY CELEBRATION, 1944

On Osgood Gaston Hayes' 69th birthday, he, his three brothers, and their families enjoy the day together. *Back:* The daughters of each of the four brothers stand behind their fathers. Osgood's daughter, Louise Hayes Williams, is fifth from left. *Middle, from left:* Bob Hayes, Jack Hayes, Osgood Hayes, and Brown Hayes. *Front:* Osgood's grandchildren, James "Jim" and Betty Williams

OSGOOD GASTON HAYES, CIRCA 1930
Always a reflective man, Osgood wrote his thoughts about life in his poetry. Some of his poems are included in this book.

RUTH ELIZABETH WILLIAMS HAYES, CIRCA 1930
Beloved wife of Osgood Gaston Hayes and mother of Louise Hayes Williams, Ruth exemplified virtuous Christian character and excellent homemaking skills.

25th WEDDING ANNIVERSARY, 1950

The Williams family celebrate Ernest and Louise's 25th wedding anniversary. *From left*: Louise Hayes Williams, James Ernest Williams, Jr., Betty Louise Williams, James Ernest Williams, Sr.

40th WEDDING ANNIVERSARY, OCTOBER 1965
James Ernest and Louise Hayes Williams celebrate their 40th wedding anniversary in Atlanta.

CHANDLERS MOVE TO NEW JERSEY, 1971
Williams-Chandler family members gather before the Chandlers move from Atlanta to New Jersey. *Back, from left*: Eddie Chandler, Sr.; Ernest Williams; Louise Hayes Williams. *Middle, from left*: John Chandler, Ezzie Chandler, James Williams, James Chandler. *Front, from left*: Eddie Chandler, Jr.; Betty Chandler; Carol Chandler *(Olan Mills photo)*

HALL OF FAME, CIRCA 1980

The Williams family celebrate William Percy Williams' induction into the University of Tennessee's School of Journalism Hall of Fame. Percy (died, 1970) was a West Tennessee newspaper editor and brother of Ernest Williams. *From left:* Bill Russ, Jimmy Williams, Carol Russ, Louise Williams, and Dorothy Williams

FRIENDS FOREVER, 1987
From left: Ezzie Webb Chandler
and Louise Hayes Williams,
grandmothers of Carol Chandler Russ,
share a moment in a friendship
of nearly fifty years.

**MOTHER AND DAUGHTER,
CIRCA 1988**
From left: Betty Williams Chandler
and mother, Louise Hayes Williams

AT BAT, 1999

The grandchildren and great-grandchildren of Louise Hayes Williams enjoy touring the Louisville (Ky.) Slugger Museum.

Back, from left: Cathy Chandler, Caileigh Chandler, Mark Russ, John Chandler, Jim Chandler, James Williams, Jr. *Front, from left*: David Russ, Carol Russ, Christin Chandler, Kathy Chandler, Betty Chandler

RUSS FAMILY, 1993
From left: Mark William Russ, Carol Chandler Russ, William Eldon Russ, David Chandler Russ (Olan Mills photo)

MARK AND LAUREN RUSS FAMILY, 2014
William and Carol Chandler Russ's son Mark and family:
Mark and Lauren Ilene Russ and their daughters
From left, Rebekah Russ and Abigail Russ

DAVID AND DEANDRA RUSS FAMILY, 2015

William and Carol Chandler Russ' son David and family: David Chandler and Deandra Leigh Russ and their daughter Eliora Russ

ACROSS THE GENERATIONS, 2015
William and Carol Russ' granddaughters, Abigail Catherine Russ *(left)* and her sister, Rebekah Lynn Russ, lovingly admire their baby cousin, Eliora Kathryn Russ. Louise Hayes Williams was their great-great grandmother. Their paternal grandmother, Carol Chandler Russ, compiled this volume and dedicated it to them.

"We're rich in the things that count!"

--- Louise Hayes Williams

BOY DREAMS
To my five-year-old son, Jim

Two chubby little arms on the window sill,
With gaze turned upward at a plane in sight,
His eyes took on a new wondrous light,
"Mommy," he mused, "someday I'll fly!"

I wondered as I watched his enchanted gaze
Till darkness covered o'er the sun's last rays
With a blanket designed with the stars
    and the moon
And I knew from his eyes he'd grown big
    too soon –
Just yesterday I rocked him bye.

Dream on, little fellow, of what you will do,
Many flyers at your age probably flew, too,
Many a man has followed the beam,
That held him fast from a boyhood dream –
Who knows – someday you too, little Jim,
    may fly.

1945
Age 43

A TRIP TO SEE SANTA CLAUS

With dishes unwashed and beds unmade,
A turkey to prepare, I was awfully afraid
We wouldn't see Santa Claus.
I was tired, in fact, I was really weary,
Presents to wrap – of course, I was leery,
I couldn't afford a pause.

I looked at Jim and his eyes were bright,
They seemed to shine like a starry night.
So, I stopped in the middle of doing
   my things.
We buttoned up warm for the trip to town,
He thrilled and chattered all the way down
With the thrill that childhood brings.

Santa was gone, but his things were there
In Jim's excitement, I felt my share
And it stirred me deep in my soul.
Because he was happy, I was satisfied.

His very first question, he asked with pride,
"Mommy, is this the North Pole?"
The house could go, with food uncooked,
For into a little boy's heart I had looked,
As I held his hand in mine.
How glad I was that I dropped everything.
It helped me to hear the angels sing.
It gave me a glow divine.

Circa 1945

MY GIFTS TO CHRIST AT CHRISTMAS

Now, I'll prepare my gifts for Christ,
The gold, the frankincense and myrrh.
I will not wrap them in packages fine,
But present them as once they were.

A sense of worship, I'll hold in my heart,
As I bring to Him my gold.
A star, a stable, and a newborn King,
Once led the wise men of old.

I will bring to Him the fragrance of life
In my gift of frankincense.
The wise men gave the gift of themselves
As Christians have sought to since
    Christ's time.

The myrrh, I will give in a spirit of faith
And I will pack it with an added grace.
I think I shall put it with the frankincense
As I lay my gifts in place.

Undated

TO HAVE A FRIEND
To my friend Ruth

To have a friend is to feel a glow
In a darkened world of doubt
When we can't decide the way to go,
There's a guiding hand held out.

To have a friend is to feel secure
In the cluttered confusion of life.
'Tis good to know someone for sure
Will help to clear the strife!

To have a friend is steady growth
Of the soul as of the mind.
The state of friendship stimulates both
One's best a friend will find.

Friendship moves the spirit on wings
To attain the utmost height.
It clothes in beauty everyday things
And makes the world seem right.

Feb. 01, 1945
Age 42

MY MORNING PRAYER

Dear God, as I begin my day
With all my heart and soul I pray
That I may see and feel the beauty
In what I sometimes feel is duty;
And with an added interest keen,
Prepare me for Thy great Unseen –
This dear Father, I pray.

And as I go about each task,
Dear Father, I do sincerely ask
Thy strength, for Thou dost know how weak
I am, and so I humbly seek
Thy touch in all the things I do;
I want to walk along with you –
Go with me, God, this day.

As night draws near and day is done
In the glory of Thy setting sun,
Let me have no feelings of regret
For which, in the night, I'd toss and fret,
But, give me a peace which only Thou canst give,
And a knowledge of how Thou hadst me live
This, dear Father, I pray.

Feb. 09, 1945
Age 42

MY GARDEN PATHS

The three little paths short
    And yet they adventure far.
They lead from the gift of a rosebud
    To the very farthermost star.

In memory one travels to the past,
    As it carries a red rose
Of love and cherished memories
    That only sentiment knows.

One goes in my everyday word
    And gives my spirit a lift, O Lord!
For it began in the heart of a rose
    So, I feel in my heart, the gift.

One reaches into the future
    Like wings in an unknown flight,
But a single rose of red
    Will give days more light.

1945
Age 43

MY LOVES

I love the sky and the tall pine trees,
The sun by the lake and
   the pleasant breeze,
The birds that sing from morn until night,
They tell me wrongs will turn to right.

I own the challenge the new day brings,
As it carries me along with a heart
   that sings;
And when I'm blue on a lonesome day –
I've learned to feel it was meant that way.

I love the shadows of the late afternoon
They say the shades of night will fall soon
To bring the rest to a harried world,
Giving calm for confusion of its dizzy whirl.

I'm intrigued with magic of what
    tomorrow will be
Of unknown beauties I have yet to see,
Of little side roads where I shall go,
Of surprises I'll find that I didn't know.

I love the comradeship deep and fine
With an understanding friend
    whom I'll call mine
Who helps me to see the beauty of a thing
And the song in my heart bursts forth
    to sing.

1945
Age 43

I WISH FOR YOU

A desire for solitude – to have it fulfilled,
Outbursts of emotion – to suddenly be stilled
By a force from within – that brings you
    peace,
Causing your soul to know increase,
And ringing you more of understanding,
    dear –
These wishes are mine for you this year.

A tear in your eye o'er a silly thing,
And a smile of courage
    for disappointment's sting,
A little of bitterness – and a spirit
    that's low –
Yet, strong to rise, till you feel all aglow,
With the fullness of joy at meeting
    the test –
Conquering, presenting your ultimate best.

A thrill o'er a flower that blooms for you,
And an ache for a friend that you
    thought untrue,
To find you were wrong – you have him still,
To continue as comrade, and with you fulfill
These wishes of mine for your own
    New Year
I wish you the fullness of life, my dear.

Undated

THE ROSE OF FRIENDSHIP
*Composed at 2 a.m. while I was waiting
for my family to come home*

I looked in the heart of a rose one day
    To find its fragrance rare,
And I knew each petal, tho' torn apart
    Must give to the rose its share.

I looked in the soul of a friend today,
    And I knew she, like the rose,
Was a sweet composite of all she'd touch
    As the petals of her life she chose.

Back to the world she's giving herself
    In fragrance, like the roses sweet;
By gleaning the best and giving it forth
    She's building a life complete.

March 17, 1946
Age 43

CONTENT

I made a search for happiness –
    a state that isn't found,
The void that came with searching
    Kept my spirit bound.

I closed my eyes to envision,
    By the best of my heart instead,
And then I made a discovery,
    Content, by the heart, is bred.

Happiness is all about me,
    I can look around and see,
I had its prison in my heart –
    But now I've set it free.

1946
Age 44

RELEASE

God, You answered my prayer for peace,
You made my nervous unrest cease,
Now I can give the world my best,
All is clear within my breast –
   For I'm in touch with You.

I lost my gleam for a little while,
I must have forgotten that I'm Your child,
Because I floundered and was ill at ease,
Perhaps I forgot how You can appease –
   If only we come to You.

The things that upset were ever so small,
But to You, in prayer, I brought them all,
I knew that You would understand,
And tighten Your grip upon my hand –
   I'll always come to You!

1946
Age 44

LIFE'S SEA

*Inspired by a sermon
by Dr. Monroe F. Swilley, pastor,
Second Ponce de Leon
Baptist Church, Atlanta, Georgia*

Forgive me, God, that I hug the shore
    In my own sweet self-content.
I'm ready to launch into the deep
    With vision from Heaven sent.

There's more to life than I have known
    Of suffering and of woe;
There's much to do for Jesus' sake,
    To Him, my love I'll show.

I'll forge into the unknown deep,
    And safer, I will be
As I set my sails in Jesus' name,
    On life's uncharted sea.

No longer will I hug the shore
    Along some shallow place,
And as I launch into the deep
    I'll see my Master's face.

1947
Age 45

BLESSED ARE GOD'S OWN
*Aliae Sunday School class devotional,
Second Ponce de Leon Baptist Church,
Atlanta, Georgia*

Blessed are the pure in heart,
    For God is theirs to see,
The magic wonder of His love,
    Shall thru the ages be.

And thru the hearts of men on earth,
    God's love shall ever flow,
His Kingdom we shall help to gain,
    Because we love Him so.

But first, we must be right inside,
    With conscience free of sin,
Then, in our sweet communion,
    We can let the Master in.

When in our hearts we've felt Him,
    We must not keep Him there,
But as a fountain flows for all,
    With others we must share.

Tis then we've seen our Savior,
    And filled our deepest need,
To cause another to see Him
    Is seeing God indeed.

1947
Age 45

THANK YOU, GOD, FOR LIFE
To Mary Hardy
after an inspiring conversation

We thank you, God, for the breadth of life,
    That reaches far away,
Down the lonely road to the stranger's gate
    We want to learn the way –
The lonely and the sad are everywhere,
    Perhaps next door to me;
Help me, God, to expand my life,
    That I may honor Thee.

We thank you, God, for the depth of life,
    For the stillness of the night,
It is only thru knowing darkness,
    That we value the dawn of light;
The gloom is often frightening,
    And we feel a deep despair,
But You can lift us from the depth,
    For we know how much You care.

We thank you, God, for the heights
    That lift our souls to Thee,
For the lofty thoughts and deeds
    That forever and ever shall be.
For the baby's smile, the bird's sweet note,
    And the flowers in the spring,
For faith in today and hope for tomorrow –
    That only You can bring.

March 11, 1949
Age 46

SOLVING PROBLEMS

In what does true success consist –
    Must it be houses and land to hold?
Is failure promoted by ones we've missed
    While striving for our goal?

Does Principle play any part?
    Does honor hold its own?
Is truth seen on Life's chart
    Where mercy and justice are shown?

Is worldly wealth the greatest power?
    May we trust it from day to day?
Are we growing richer each hour
    In treasures that with us stay?

Does fair dealing have its appeal?
    Can we live by the golden rule?
May we the rights of our neighbors shield
    And to the many good things hold true?

Are there many worthwhile things
    Proving worthy of time and place?
Shall these much joy to us bring
    When their real meaning we trace?

These questions to us are given
    For solution – each one in his way
When we have heartily striven
    They will all be answered day by day.

Undated

TO BETTY
ON MOTHER'S DAY 1954
FROM MOTHER

One month prior to this Mother's Day, my daughter Betty gave birth to her first child nine weeks prematurely. Little Barbara Louise Chandler, my first grandchild, lived only three days.

You're a little nearer Heaven,
There's a bit of you up there,
God keeps you a little closer
For He gave you an extra share.

You belong to His anointed,
Who live for Him each day
He watches over you tenderly
Along your everyday way.

Your sharing with Ed is rich
God's present in all you do
A brand new day is dawning –
A good day for you.

Mother's Day 1954
Age 51

TO RISE AGAIN

I sat by the tomb of my dreams
    And wrapped myself in my woe;
In the gloom of my disappointment,
    Not a spark of hope did I know.

I was still as I sat there mourning
    In the quiet of the early dawn.
Then, I heard a voice saying clearly,
    "Arise, your woes are gone."

I looked up, and the sun was shining,
    The blossoms had burst into bloom,
The earth had an aura of splendor
    And brightness replaced the gloom.

So, I walked among the flowers
    Gathering blossoms as I went,
And will share with my fellow travelers
    The beauty that God had sent.

Undated

GROWTH

From the depth of my soul
New pleasures unfold
    To increase my capacity there.
I have suffered some
And thru it have come
    To understand it more, and to share.

Before, I had thought
As I earnestly sought
    To feel as the other fellow did;
But how I could know
That he'd suffered so
    When his sufferings, he always hid.

It's a little strange
How lives arrange
    In a pattern of balance, so true.
For every trouble
There are blessings double
    If we look for the good side, too.

Undated

LEAVE IT WITH HIM

Who are we to question
    The meaning of His plan?
Why not leave it with Him,
    It's too much for Man!

Our will may seem important.
    But after all, it's small.
It may mix up the pattern,
    It may not fit at all.

So why not leave it with Him
    To work out, as He will?
It's only then that peace comes
    And bids our heart be still.

Undated

"I am glad to live in America.... This is the heritage that is ours from the fathers who fought to make it so."

--Louise Hayes Williams

I AM GLAD TO LIVE IN AMERICA

I AM GLAD TO LIVE in America, the land of today, where there is ever the opportunity for a new beginning, regardless of failures or successes of the past. An American can forge into the future with plans, and apply them in confidence, for this is truly a land of opportunity.

I am a grandmother who can look backward through memories to my own grandmother, who had a great influence on my early years. Also, I can look forward through the excitement of my small granddaughter into a life which will surely be filled with new and interesting things. It will hold challenge, hope, and attainment. This span of confidence through the generations makes America truly a land of the free.

In America we are free to work and earn, as we are free to save and have, we are free to give and take and apply the Golden Rule. We are free to come and go, to start and stop as we please, so long as we do not interfere with the rights of others. We are allowed to use our best choices for our own lives and, through service groups, are privileged to give our better selves to the betterment of mankind. Our greatest freedom is our ability to worship as we please.

We are free to help make and execute the laws of our land. Our democracy allows a close touch with our government, thereby making each man a partner in it. Nowhere else on earth is there the freedom which I enjoy in my country.

There is strength in America, for which every citizen may well be proud – strength of manpower, finance, and of product. It is a rich country, having natural resources which enable man to be self-sustaining. There is strength in the soil and the ore, on the land and in the sea. Commodities are ours in such quantity that we enjoy comfortable living as no other country does. We have learned from our pioneer fathers that life has become safer, stronger, and easier. We have converted much of our energy toward research and development because machines are doing so much of our labor and menial work. The ever-developing research is giving our nation an enviable place in world affairs, and, of course, with it, influence.

Our youth are developing projects in science, productions in the arts; and nowhere is there a place of greater opportunities for our youth. Our fast-growing field of medical research is changing our nation's health standard. Our people are living longer, enjoying life more, and becoming each day, a healthier nation. We are strong.

There is beauty in America that makes life more thrilling. From the mountains to the seas, there are magnificent roadways beckoning man to see its wonders. Air flight has become an everyday commodity for travel and sightseeing. People of all levels of life have equal opportunity for seeing the country's beauty, whether it be near or far. They can enjoy its shrines, its parks, and its developments. So much of the beauty is free.

We live comfortably in America. Through scientific advances, we are able to use less time and effort in our work, thereby having more time and energy for recreation. We can enjoy life's extras, which make for happier living. Methods of communication make us a closely knit nation – close to our relatives, our friends, and our business opportunities.

Transportation is a commodity for which we can be proud. In America there are so many places to go and so many ways to get there.

Our markets take care of all our needs and wants. We have equal opportunities for receiving an education, for realizing an income through our effort, and for creating financial security through our management. In America, one can have almost any kind of life he chooses.

In our democracy there is the opportunity for those who wish to have homes of their own and enjoy the American way of life in all its richness. My family lives simply, yet elegantly. Though our income is small, we can live with great music and literature. Through means of television, we can visit with the great world figures until we feel we know them personally. We can have our friends into our homes to enjoy our blessings with us or we can close our doors with privacy.

In America there are homes of all types. There are streets of small homes where young people can start their family and their lives independently with economic safety. There are country communities of scattered homes. All of life in this land comes out of the heart of its homes. Its people are urged by society to make those homes happy ones. The people mingle together in religion, in business, in education, in recreation and in travel. They touch each other in happiness, in sorrow, and in adventure. They learn as tiny children to live together in groups, regardless of where they live. They are brought together in many areas through our efficient means of transportation. They work and learn and play together. There is no age limit on learning. A grandmother and a teenager may both attend college.

Then, when the day is over and when the people are tired, they can return home for an evening of their choosing. It is good when we have expended energy in the day's activities to return home for rest and understanding. There, we need no longer to keep up a front, we can close out the world if we like, and enjoy the quiet and privacy of our own world. This freedom alone is sufficient to express what it means to be an American. There is so much vigorous living, it is good to retreat at intervals to store up more energy for another try at getting all we can out of this wonderful world. Even our smallest homes have benefit of the wonders of our age.

This is the heritage that is ours from the fathers who fought to make it so.

Undated

*"Develop courage
to try."*

--Louise Hayes Williams

TOWARD A SUCCESSFUL LIFE

1. KEEP THE SPIRIT OF GOD in your heart. Ask for and follow His guidance. In all relations and activities, be aware of your Maker.

2. Enjoy the satisfaction of work and a job well-done – day by day.

3. Keep the respect of your fellowman by being responsible, trustworthy, and fair. An old phrase says it well, "Tote square."

4. Value your credit – do not abuse it. Use it only for what you can pay when it is due.

5. Protect your health – it is your most valuable asset. If control, restraint, and consultation are required to manage it, these are your best investments.

6. Keep informed. The way of life is constant change, but learn what and when not to change. Keep your way and values in order.

7. Communicate your views, your thinking, your ideas, your knowledge, and your feelings with understanding persons. Study the personalities of those to whom you confide so there will be no reasons for regret.

8. Develop courage to try. If one ventures and fails, try again in another field.

9. Search out other persons' abilities and help promote them to accomplishment ... and yourself.

10. Bank for your future even a dollar a day. Opportunity may knock when you least expect it.

Undated

"As I see it, our God-given talents are ours, for God's whole purpose in our lives."

--Louise Hayes Williams

A PRAYER FROM THE HEART OF A MOTHER
Written at 3:30 a.m.

MAY I BE GIVEN enough time, past this age eighty-two, to realize some of the dreams I have borne in my heart and bared to my Father in heaven regarding my children, whom I love so much. I have lived to see them as Christian believers, with their faith in God and a joy in His works. I trust that He will direct them into using their talents for their own sakes and the sakes of others.

As I see it, our God-given talents are ours, for God's whole purpose in our lives. Here on earth we are preparing for the Better Life. This world is a training ground where we prove ourselves as responsible persons, exhibiting God's spirit, and at the same time, fitting into the work pattern of life. This is where our varied talents are needed.

I believe that God created us male and female for the purpose of propagating the population of the world. In this process, He gave to babies and little children the love and warmth of a mother's caring when it was needed, training and helping guide them to a special place in the world. For the male children, it has always been the custom to educate them toward productive work, with income to fill their needs.

Many feel called to the ministry of God's Word. Many have prepared and offered the effectual training for this work. It is not necessary to do His work as a livelihood in order to live in a world of financial requirements. One's work-a-day life can be enhanced by volunteer giving, but the work makes it necessary to be able to give to those who need help. Great satisfaction comes to those who do a good day's work. He uses his ability, his strength, and is better able to help those who cannot work.

I thank you, Dear Father, for the wonderful opportunity to feed our family when my husband Ernest could no longer work. I thank Thee this did not happen until my children could prepare for life. I may soon be gone and my most earnest prayer now is they and theirs will always be self-supporting, do their good deeds, and someday we will reunite in a Better World.

1985
Age 82

PART TWO

THE COLLECTED POETRY

OF

OSGOOD GASTON HAYES

(Born May 25, 1875, Georgia;
Died May 22, 1953, Atlanta, Georgia)

WHO WAS OSGOOD HAYES?
By Carol Chandler Russ

THE ATLANTA STREETCAR came to a halt as the flow of electricity stopped on a late spring day in 1943. The passengers included Osgood Gaston Hayes. As he and the others waited for the electricity to resume, Osgood was overcome with the powerful sense that Ruth, his beloved wife of forty-three years, had departed this earthly life. "Memie's gone," he exclaimed.

When he reached the family home in south Atlanta, Osgood found that his premonition was true. In fact, his family confirmed that the very moment of the power failure on the street car was the same moment that Ruth had died. Over the years since, his family – including myself as his great-granddaughter – has often pondered the fact that given his closeness to the Lord, perhaps the Lord imparted supernatural knowledge to him that day.

Throughout his life, Osgood did possess an unusual spiritual sensitivity, as evidenced by this and other stories told by his family and friends. He was known as a quiet and gentle man, very reflective. His poetry included in this volume attests to that.

For many years, Osgood worked in the store owned by his brother, Brown Hayes. As he stocked store shelves, he must have had time to think and reflect on life. Surely, he encountered many types of people as they came to shop. Meditating on the characteristics of the people he met, coupled with plenty of time to think, seems to have given rise to his poetry. Surely he offered gentle words of wisdom to shoppers as well. Poems such as "Things That Abide" and "The Day's Investments" seem to have grown out of those experiences.

Osgood always loved nature – birds, trees, flowers, squirrels – and often took long nature walks. He enjoyed hunting, fishing, and roaming the woods as a boy.

He also deeply loved his family of three brothers – Brown, Jack, and Bob – and sister Merle. He was very close to his daughter and only child, Ruth Louise Hayes, and his quiet, shy granddaughter, Betty Louise Williams — my mother.

Osgood died in Atlanta in 1953, ten years after his beloved wife, Ruth. As a great-granddaughter born two years after his death, I am thankful for his skill with the pen. I am thankful that I may know of his heart even though I never heard his voice. May readers enjoy his deep reflections and the spirituality of his poetry.

MERELY A DREAM

Recently in a vivid dream
    One that proved very pleasing
Much rich treasure it did seem
    Time spent well for its seizing.

A lonely place upon a hill
    Of almost desolation
Such treasure my heart would fill
    By its welcome visitation.

Bags of silver, yea pots of gold,
    Unearthed to view above the clay
This shining metal to behold
    Meant welcome to a better day.

My own self I'll help while here;
    Flesh is lean and clothes are bare
Then others in the find will share.
    Many children will better share.

Still gazing on the wondrous scene
    One to move the slowest heart.
Ambition now had grown so keen
    To have the needy share a part.

Alone on this mountain spot
   Amazed by so rich a find
Life has been hard, I thought,
   I shall here cease a daily grind.

To guard the prize means to tarry,
   Couldn't afford to leave it alone.
Neither to remove nor carry,
   Its bulk too heavy to be bourne.

At length I looked – it precious grew
   Why should I now bestow my own?
I've played my part – let others do –
   I'll gladly reap the labors sown.

The thought of others in the find
   For aid had now been banished.
Wealth's changing power had fixed the mind
   Each one had paled and vanished.

Awakening from this transient spell
   A thrilling dream was quick to tell,
Wealth in imagination's grasp
   Typical of Life – 'tis quickly passed.

THE DAY'S INVESTMENTS

The old day now is past
   The new one soon will dawn
May we see in its cast
   New hopes with courage form.

Yes – succeeding ones must be
   Made better than the old
Making heavy hearts more free
   From obstructions to their goal.

Where thoughts and inspirations blend
   Forming ambitious ways to tread,
The fondest dreams are realized
   And thoughts of failure fled.

Each cheerful word we've spoken
   To the discouraged on the way
Has been the purest token
   Of our spirit for the day.

Nothing good is ever lost
   But treasured with the days;
Good works merit any cost
   In their many varied ways.

THE NEW DAY

The old day now is past.
    A new one will soon dawn.
May it show happy cast
    Of endeavors yet unborn.

Yes, succeeding ones must each
    Prove better than the old.
When eager hands may reach
    Successful stretches for a goal.

Progress will ever blaze the trail
    As pilot to the safer way.
The steps alert may never fail
    In hopeful gain of future day.

No other means can measure
    The loss and profits of a day
Than ones in which we treasure
    More hopeful aspects on the way.

Though far-flung at our very door
    A future likeness we may see
Our personnel in coming lore,
    As each one may decree.

THE SIGNIFICANT HAND

The hand of love outstretched
    Will steer from danger's roughed ways
Guiding the feet through beauty sketched
    From fairest sunlit rays.

This hand to lead through gardens fair
    Where peaceful days abide.
And in the fields of culture rare
    No happy feet shall step aside.

This pulsating hand of love
    Throbbing for a healthy clasp,
Beckoning, imploring to serve
    Undertaking its noble task.

Groping in darkness till we feel
    This cordial hand extended wide,
Tightened by a grip and shield
    As though our angel guide.

Through pastures rich with meadows green
    Where little brooks go rushing by
Shadows dark are never seen
    For fairer lands, never a sigh.

This hand must point toward ideals fair
    Leading in all its councils wise,
Lifting the souls from earthly care
    And who, its significance shall prize.

THINGS THAT ABIDE

Twas something said or done today
    That lingered long,
Helping to brighten someone's way,
    By word or song.

A kindly act was done,
    By you or me,
A grateful friend was won
    And true was he.

While on a long and lonely road
    A helping hand,
Relieved him of a tiresome load,
    That he might stand.

He may not see the face again,
    Nor grasp the hand
That helped relieve the burdened brain
    And troubles ban
But thru future days that come and go,
    He'll never forget
The friend who greatly helped him through
    He'll cherish yet.

ABOUT THE AUTHORS

RUTH LOUISE HAYES WILLIAMS was born in rural Greene County, Georgia on Aug. 01, 1902. She married Ernest Williams on Oct. 07, 1925. For the first twenty-five years of their marriage, Louise – as she was known – was a stay-at-home wife and mother of two children, Betty and Jim. She was also an active volunteer in her church and community.

After Ernest suffered two debilitating heart attacks and could no long work, Louise joined the work force to support her family. She worked in the Atlanta school system and then became director of Diabetes Association of Atlanta, a United Way agency.

She died in Atlanta at age ninety, sixteen years after her husband's death.

OSGOOD GASTON HAYES, Louise Hayes Williams' father, was born in Georgia in 1875. He died in Atlanta in 1953.

CAROL CHANDLER RUSS is the only granddaughter of Louise Hayes Williams and the only great-granddaughter of Osgood Gaston Hayes. In 2016, Carol and her husband, Bill, live in Louisville, Kentucky.

www.ingramcontent.com/pod-product-compliance
Lightning Source LLC
Chambersburg PA
CBHW051653040426
42446CB00009B/1111